Original title:
Echoes in the Evergreen Glade

Copyright © 2025 Creative Arts Management OÜ
All rights reserved.

Author: Jameson Hartfield
ISBN HARDBACK: 978-1-80567-446-7
ISBN PAPERBACK: 978-1-80567-745-1

Nature's Harmonious Soliloquy

In the woods where frogs croak loud,
A squirrel's antics reclaim the crowd.
Leaves whisper secrets, so sly,
While raccoons plan their late-night fry.

Breezes tickle tree branches wide,
As chipmunks play peekaboo, they hide.
Nature laughs, a merry tune,
Under the watch of the glowing moon.

The Poetics of Leaf and Light

Sunbeams dance on petals bright,
While ants march on with all their might.
A butterfly flits without a care,
As if to say, just stop and stare!

The grumpy owl, with a frown so grand,
Hoots a rhythm, it's poorly planned!
The chattering birds sing out a song,
Nature's party where all belong.

Sibilant Sentiments of the Swamps

Marsh a-muck with a croaky cheer,
A gator slumps, "I need a beer!"
Dragonflies buzz with gossip grand,
While cattails sway, a dancing band.

Frogs in tuxedos leap and slide,
While crickets strum, they won't abide.
It's a swamp soirée, a wild spree,
Where mud is the dress code, come join the glee!

Portraits of a Living Canopy

Trees wear hats, they're quite the show,
With fungi smiles that always glow.
A vine comes creeping, oh what a sight,
Making sure it ties the party tight!

Birds in bow ties start to squawk,
While woodpeckers do their knocking talk.
Every branch tells a funny plot,
In this jungle, the laughter's caught.

The Light Between the Oaks

In the shade where squirrels play,
A frog croaks tunes in a funny way.
Leaves wiggle like they've lost their tune,
While birds shake their feathers' morning gloom.

A rabbit hops with such a flair,
He stops to pose, as if unaware.
The sun beams down, it starts to dance,
And every critter joins in their prance.

Harmony in the Grove

The woodpecker drummed out a silly song,
While butterflies fluttered, all so strong.
A chipmunk juggles acorns with pride,
As laughter of leaves swirls far and wide.

An owl hoots with a wink in his eye,
As the busy bumblebee buzzes by.
The trees bend low, sharing a grin,
Like they know where all the mischief begins.

Revelations From the Rooted Depths

From deep below, the worms convene,
To swap wild tales of the grass they've seen.
With little giggles, they share their plight,
Of dodging raindrops in the soft twilight.

The daisies gossip, petals aflutter,
While ants march by, straight to the clutter.
A root tickles, a sprout gives a wink,
In this green realm, nothing's as it seems.

Fen and Foliage Murmuration

In the fen, the cattails play hide and seek,
While frogs on logs exchange funny speak.
Amidst the foliage, shadows leap and twirl,
As pesky gophers do the rabbit whirl.

The dragonflies joke, zooming so fast,
While turtles chuckle, moving at last.
Every breeze brings a chuckle or two,
In this woodland scene, so lively and true.

Reverie of the Glistening Glade

In the woods where whispers play,
Squirrels chat and lions sway.
They joke about the size of trees,
And giggle at the buzzing bees.

Rabbits wear their Sunday best,
While birds complain about the nest.
Frogs join in with ribbit tunes,
Underneath the laughing moons.

Mice dance on the mushrooms' cap,
While slugs take part in slowest tap.
All the critters laugh and cheer,
Announcing spring is finally here!

Nature's jest is loud and clear,
With every bounce and every cheer.
In this realm of leafy sprites,
Laughter flows in endless flights.

Tones of Twilight Among the Pines

Amidst the pines, a party brews,
A raccoon moonlights in his shoes.
He juggles acorns, what a sight,
While owls hoot with pure delight.

Bats above play tag in flight,
While fireflies flicker late at night.
The trees are swaying to their tune,
As crickets sing and charm the moon.

A fox in shades tells clever jokes,
The hedgehogs giggle; here come the blokes!
A breeze carries their joyful sound,
As laughter echoes all around.

Among the pines, a mischief thrives,
Where nature's whimsy truly thrives.
In twilight tones, the fun won't stop,
For every critter's ready to bop!

Whispers of the Hidden Woods

In the woods where stories buzz,
Silly tales and playful fuzz.
A bear wears glasses just to see,
And grins at squirrels high in trees.

Frogs recite their poems loud,
While giggly rabbits form a crowd.
Together they share funny lore,
As branches sway and creatures roar.

Woodpeckers knock a silly beat,
While turtles try to dance on feet.
All the logs begin to rock,
Creating games without a clock.

With every whisper, laughter grows,
In hidden glades where joy just flows.
Nature's winks and cheeky grins,
In playful woods, the laughter spins.

Shadows Dance in the Thicket

Within the thicket, shadows tease,
A cat that sneezes, oh what a breeze!
The raccoons laugh and tell a tale,
Of a fish that tries to peddle mail.

A hedgehog spins in quite a whirl,
While mice dress up in pearls and twirl.
They plan a party under the stars,
Where even the owls clap for the mars.

Bats play hide and seek with glee,
While slugs take selfies near the tree.
Their laughter mixes with the night,
In shadows dancing, pure delight.

Nature's frolic, wild and free,
A true gathering, don't you see?
In thickets dark, where mirth ignites,
The world's a stage for funny sights.

Voices of the Wildwood

In the woods where squirrels chatter,
A rabbit wears a top hat, mad as a hatter.
Birds gossip of seeds, shiny and round,
While ants march in lines, oh what a sound!

Trees shrug their branches, thick with delight,
As shadows play tag until the last light.
A bear does the cha-cha, all paws in a dance,
While the fox takes a bow, giving life a chance.

The wind pulls a prank, tickles the leaves,
As the owl hoots softly, "How clever he weaves!"
Mushrooms giggle as they sprout from the ground,
In this wild, wildwood, joy abound!

So wander, dear friend, where laughter is free,
With critters conspiring in mischievous glee.
Underneath the old oaks, let your troubles slide,
In the heart of the wildwood, take a wild ride!

Melodies of the Soft Earth

In the glen where the daisies sway with grace,
A snail plays the trumpet at a leisurely pace.
Frogs join in chorus, croaking away,
While the bees buzz along, in perfect display.

The grass tickles toes, making laughter ensue,
As daisies spin tales of an old, quirky brew.
Feathered friends mimic the sounds they all glean,
Creating a symphony of silly and keen.

A hedgehog in shades rolls by with a grin,
Wiggling his quills, trying to win.
The earthworms are grooving, deep down in the muck,
Plotting a flash mob, oh what luck!

Come dance with the daisies, be part of the fun,
In this realm of the soft earth, joy has begun.
Nature's sweet melodies, a whimsical fate,
In laughter and music, let's celebrate!

The Tree's Silent Testimony

Old oak stands tall, a witness to jest,
As raccoons race up, vying for best.
Branches shake softly with secrets they hold,
Of rambunctious squirrels and mischief bold.

A woodpecker's tapping, a rhythm quite fine,
While rabbits debate which patch is divine.
With a wink and a nudge, they scatter and rustle,
The tree chuckles lightly at their little hustle.

With roots deep in laughter and leaves in the breeze,
The old tree keeps tales of treasures with ease.
Whispers of giggles linger high in the air,
Serenade of the forest, beyond all compare.

So lean close to the bark, hear the stories unfold,
Of creatures that frolic, both timid and bold.
In nature's sweet presence, let your spirit glide,
For the tree's silent whispers, will be your guide!

Cadence of the Calm Clearing

In a clearing so bright, the sun shines anew,
A frog in a tutu leads the dancers askew.
Bunnies hop wildly, they twirl and they spin,
While the daisies all cheer, "Let the fun begin!"

The breeze whirls around in a playful embrace,
As butterflies flutter in a whimsical race.
The grasshoppers strum on their fiddles with cheer,
Creating a tune for all critters to hear.

The owls tell tall tales with a wink of an eye,
While ants throw a party, oh my, oh my!
A hedgehog spins tales of wonder and glee,
Unfolding the laughter in this bright jubilee.

So gather your friends, join the merry parade,
In this calm clearing where joy isn't delayed.
Nature's grand festival, where humor prevails,
In the cadence of laughter, life never pales!

Alchemy of Nature's Symphony

In the woods where squirrels dance,
A raccoon stole my lunch, what a chance!
The birds sing tunes like a choir gone mad,
While I chase my snack, feeling quite bad.

Leaves rustle secrets, a giggle or two,
A chipmunk gives me a peek, what to do?
The trees hold their laughter with every breeze,
And I trip on a root, down on my knees.

Frogs croak their jokes, in a nightly reprise,
Whispering dung beetles roll laughter with ease.
With each step I take, a new mishap spins,
Nature's pranks make me chuckle, oh where do I begin?

So here in this glade, beneath sunlight's show,
I laugh with the critters, both high and low.
Life's a lighthearted jest, beneath leafy screens,
As I dance with nature, living in dreams.

Scents and Shadows of Ferns

In the thicket where shadows play,
I smell a scent that's just gone astray.
Ferns flap about like they've lost their way,
While I sniff and giggle, what a wild display!

A skunk waddles past, I hold my breath tight,
Hoping it's friendly and not looking to bite.
But then I see flowers, all colors and charms,
Laughing their petals, no need for alarms.

Mushrooms pop up, dressed for a ball,
Whispering secrets, they've seen it all.
And I trip over one, what's that smell?
Let's just say, they've cast quite the spell!

With shadows and scents that tickle my nose,
The giggles of wildlife nobody knows.
In nature's perfume, I lose track of time,
Every step is a joke—what a hill of a climb!

Breath of the Emerald Expanse

In the emerald breath where the breezes roam,
The trees tell stories, I call them my home.
As I wander and stumble with laughter loud,
A gopher pops up, looking quite proud.

With each misty hint of the forest's delight,
The rabbits are gossiping, oh what a sight!
A deer nods with wisdom, or is it disdain?
I can't quite tell, but I chuckle again.

The ferns wave like flags in a merry parade,
While raccoons prepare for their midnight escapade.
Every plant's a character, full of surprise,
Bringing smiles and chuckles, oh such clever guys!

So here in this vastness, my heart skips a beat,
With giggles and whimsy, every critter I meet.
Nature is laughter, in whispers and sighs,
In this playful expanse, what joy is no surprise!

Timeless Tales Among the Trees

In the realm where history likes to play,
The trees tell tales of a comical sway.
A raccoon in boots, pretending to strut,
While I bend to tie shoes, feeling quite cut.

With owls in glasses, studying the night,
And squirrels who debate if they've taken flight.
The branches are filled with a scholarly crew,
I can't help but giggle; oh, what a view!

A fox with a top hat, reciting his lines,
Telling jokes to the frogs, all sipping on wines.
The moonlight shines bright, the shenanigans swirl,
As nature's own comedy begins to unfurl.

So listen quite closely to stories unspun,
In the trees and the weeds, laughter's never done.
In timeless tales woven under the moon's glow,
Nature's a stage, where giggles bestow!

Rhythms of the Ancient Shrubs

In the quiet shade they dance,
The squirrels just can't help but prance.
Funky moves with nuts in tow,
Who knew trees held such a show?

With branches swaying, quite a sight,
A wise old owl joins in the fight.
He hoots a beat, they shimmy near,
While bunnies giggle without fear.

A raccoon's moonwalk steals the day,
While chipmunks cheer and join the play.
The bushes rustle, laughter flows,
Amidst the roots, the fun just grows.

So if you wander through this space,
Expect to find a joyous race.
For nature's party never ends,
With quirky critters, laughing friends.

Lingering Notes in the Woodland Air

Up in the trees, a songbird croons,
Hilarious tunes beneath the moons.
The leaves are clapping, what a sight,
As branches sway with pure delight.

A porcupine strums a prickle bass,
While ants do jazz with lots of grace.
The beetles tap in perfect beat,
A woodland band, oh what a treat!

Dance along to the buzzing sound,
Where quirky creatures can be found.
A funny frog leads in the cheer,
His leaps and skips are quite sincere.

The melody drifts on gentle air,
Reminding us that joy is rare.
In every rustle, every note,
Nature's laughter keeps us afloat.

The Rooted Refrain of Solitude

In a nook where shadows play,
A hedgehog naps the sunny day.
But what's this? A tickling breeze,
To wake him up with such unease!

He rolls and giggles, what a sight,
As daisies dance without a fright.
With worms as friends, a comic crew,
His sleepy world becomes askew.

While pondering life in tangled roots,
He hosts a bash with tiny flutes.
The ants parade in fancy wear,
With belly laughs that fill the air.

Solitude's fun, it's clear to see,
In each little rustle of harmony.
These quirky moments, full of glee,
Remind us all to just be free.

Dreams Nurtured in the Greenery

Amidst the ferns where fun begins,
A sneaky raccoon plays tricks and grins.
With acorns scattered, he starts a game,
Claiming his treasure, much to his fame.

A chattering parrot drops by to tease,
Swinging on branches with utmost ease.
"Catch me if you can!" she squawks in play,
As critters tumble throughout the day.

When twilight falls, the fireflies blink,
Summer's party makes us think.
All animals gather to share their dreams,
Of wacky adventures in sunlight beams.

So here in green, where spirits rise,
With laughter bright and playful cries.
The folly thrives in nature's care,
And every heart is light as air.

Stories Weaved in Mossy Shadows

In the grove where squirrels plot,
They may steal your snack, oh what a rot!
The mushrooms giggle, hide their face,
While giggling fairies start a race.

A toadstool dances, quite a sight,
Trying to woo a firefly's light,
But tripping over roots that tease,
He tumbles down with laugh and wheeze.

The hedgehogs wear their spiky hats,
And trade tall tales with chubby bats,
Who claim they flew through stormy skies,
Yet flopped like pancakes—what a prize!

Whispers in the twilight glow,
As moonlight gives the night a show,
In a funny glen of bouncing cheer,
Where every creature sheds a tear.

Elysian Trails Through the Thicket

Through winding paths where brambles dance,
A rabbit prances, full of chance,
He challenges the snails for fun,
As twilight glows, the race is on!

The wise old owl, with specs so round,
Keeps score of antics all around,
While badgers chuckle, paws on bellies,
Tickling each other like cheeky jellies.

Beneath the ferns, a lizard twirls,
In shadows of his scaly swirls,
He sings a song, but it's a mess,
A lark suggests some new finesse!

As laughing winds through leaves will glide,
The forest's heart beats with such pride,
For all the moments, silly and sweet,
In the thicket, life is quite the treat.

The Breath of the Timbered World

In timbered realms where breezes tickle,
Laughter bursts; it's quite the pickle!
A dancing leaf takes center stage,
As squirrels laugh at life's grand page.

The tree trunks whisper jokes on high,
While raccoons snicker, oh my, oh my!
An acorn falls, a clumsy feat,
A pinecone giggles—what a treat!

The beams of light through boughs weave tales,
Of chattering creatures amidst the gales,
Chasing shadows, with squeaks and chirps,
Turning each stumble into joyful jerks.

When twilight hums a jolly call,
The woodlands dance, embracing all,
In merry woods where laughter swirls,
Nature's pulse brings whimsical pearls.

Verses from Beneath the Bark

Deep in the wood, where secrets hide,
A beetle recites with utmost pride,
About the day he missed a meal,
And how the ants danced, oh what a deal!

The fungus shares a rather tall tale,
Of sneaky cats with ninja trails,
While old roots chuckle, turning round,
At every joke that's been profound.

The moonlit stage, a sight to see,
Where crickets croak in harmony,
Yet one young frog, with big dreams high,
Believed he could fly—oh my, oh my!

From every crevice, humor springs,
In the bark's embrace, the fun it brings,
With laughter ringing through the night,
The forest sings, all is just right.

Soliloquy of the Untamed

In forest deep, a squirrel pranced,
Chasing shadows, he danced and danced.
He tried to leap, but missed the tree,
Landing on a branch so carefree!

A rabbit chuckled, all in good cheer,
Said, "You're the dancer we all revere!"
The fox rolled his eyes with a playful grin,
"Next time, friend, let's not begin!"

Traces of Time in the Wilderness

A wise old owl began to muse,
"Each tree has tales, so many to choose!"
A beetle argued, "I'm older than you,
I've seen more than this whole forest crew!"

With branches swaying, the leaves would sway,
"Who cares," they giggled, "it's just another day!"
The sun peeked through with a playful wink,
As all the woods began to rethink!

A Symphony of Green Dreams

A frog leaped high with a boisterous croak,
"Mistress of skills, I shall invoke!"
The turtle replied with a slow-motion clap,
"Great job, dear frog, it's a curious flap!"

A breeze chimed in with a fluttering laugh,
"Shall we compose? Let's make a gaffe!"
The raccoons rolled in, with glints in their eyes,
"Count us in! We'll improvise!"

Woodland Serenades

The bumblebee buzzed, started a tune,
While daisies swayed, as if in a swoon.
A chipmunk found rhythm, and started to clap,
"Join in this jig, it's a real mishap!"

The wind spun around, giggling with glee,
"Dance, dance, everyone, come follow me!"
The mushrooms blushed, their caps in delight,
As they all partie'd until the night!

Harmony in the Shaded Haven

Beneath the leafy crown so wide,
A squirrel sat with nuts to hide.
It twirled around with zestful glee,
Chasing shadows, wild and free.

The birds debated high and loud,
While rabbits formed a furry crowd.
One got stuck in a tangle of grass,
And the others laughed as they watched him pass.

A turtle took his time to shine,
He claimed that this slow life is fine.
But when he saw the rabbit race,
He tried to speed, fell flat on his face.

The breeze sang songs, a playful tune,
As leaves danced under the bright full moon.
With every giggle that nature made,
The haven sparkled in golden shade.

Vibrations of the Leafy Sanctuary

In the grove where shadows play,
A gopher declared it his birthday.
He wore a hat made of big green leaf,
And invited all, to share in his belief.

The ants marched in, quite a sight,
Their tiny feet danced with delight.
But when they tripped on a spider's web,
They spun around, oh what a celeb!

A fox with flair brought out a drum,
He tapped it loud, then started to hum.
But every beat sent a bug on a flight,
And soon the party turned out quite bright!

The owls hooted laughter from above,
While raccoons rummaged, seeking some love.
With each silly mishap and merry spree,
The sanctuary rang with joyous glee.

Sighs Through the Tall Evergreens

Amidst tall giants, whispers swirl,
A bear with intentions to twirl.
He tripped on a twig, oh what a sight,
Spinning 'round in the fading light.

A deer sat watching, giggling loud,
As frogs leapt up, formed a wet crowd.
Each splash a joke, a comedic scene,
Nature's theater, pure and green.

A skunk called out for all to see,
He tried to dance, but fell from the tree.
The laughter echoed, fun took flight,
Even the stars grew bright that night.

Breezes chimed like chimes in hand,
As every creature joined the band.
Through all the sighs and joyous cheer,
The woods were alive, no room for fear.

The Solitude of Verdant Echoes

In the woods where silence often sings,
A porcupine acted like a king.
With a crown of thorns, he strutted around,
But stepped on a thorn and fell to the ground.

A wise old owl with a twinkling eye,
Watched all the antics and wondered why.
He hooted loudly at the sight so weird,
As all creatures gathered, their laughter cheered.

Along came a crow with wisdom to share,
"Try not to dance if you can't spare!"
Yet the rabbits hopped around with grace,
Each leap a comedy, an endless chase.

With every tumble and silly trick,
Nature's humor flowed, thick and quick.
In solitude's realm, where chuckles soar,
The verdant stage welcomed laughter galore.

Resonance of the Nature's Heart

The squirrel holds a grand old feast,
With acorns stacked like little beasts.
A raccoon joins, a masked bandit bold,
As they nibble on nuts, quite uncontrolled.

The tree bark laughs, it seems to say,
"Wear your best suit for the nutty ballet!"
While birds whistle tunes, in feathered delight,
A gap-toothed hare hops and aims for height.

Footsteps in the Emerald Wilds

A frog in a tux, quite dapper he leaps,
While a deer twirls slowly, shattering sleeps.
The light through the leaves is a playful jive,
As the winds tease the branches, keeping dreams alive.

Chubby chipmunks in dance, their tails in a whirl,
Swaying as flowers start to unfurl.
The forest giggles at their foolish grace,
As they tumble and squawk in a woodland race.

Hushed Calls of the Woodland Spirits

A wise old owl, in a top hat so grand,
Proclaims to a rabbit, "Let's start a band!"
The bushes shiver, as they join in song,
With a heavy-footed badger dancing along.

The fireflies twinkle like stars in a stir,
As they blink out rhythms and night starts to purr.
Even the shadows seem to clap and sway,
In a whimsical show where the critters play.

Beneath the Breath of the Forest

A chipmunk with style, wearing a tie,
Challenges a turtle to an all-out flyby.
They zoom through the ferns with exuberant flair,
While the trees gossip softly, a curious pair.

A clumsy old bear, stuck in a hive,
Hiccups sweet honey, making bees strive.
The laughter of nature fills up the space,
As the forest erupts in this jovial race.

Voices of Rustling Green

In the forest when I roam,
Leaves whisper secrets from their home.
Squirrels gossip in a dash,
While mushrooms giggle in a flash.

A rabbit hops with such delight,
Chatters with the frogs at night.
They argue who can jump the best,
While owls watch, amused, impressed.

The pine trees chuckle in their stance,
As crickets join the polka dance.
Bears in hats have tea, it's true,
Bananas wearing shoes join too!

Nature's jesters, loud and clear,
Sing along with widening cheer.
In this glade of silly dreams,
Laughter flows in vibrant streams.

Aerial Ballets in the Canopy

Swinging squirrels twirl with grace,
Hanging upside down, they race.
A bluebird's pirouette takes flight,
As butterflies join in the night.

A woodpecker takes center stage,
Tapping rhythms like a sage.
Leaves sway in a rhythmic tease,
While raccoons clap, 'Oh yes, please!'

A parade of ants march with pride,
Tiny legs in swift sidestide.
They're the chorus in this play,
Bringing giggles on display.

Branches sway and giggle too,
As sunlight beams in bright hues.
In this theater of delight,
Dance with shadows till the night.

Stanzas from the Underbrush

Between the brambles, whispers thrive,
Caterpillars sing, 'We're alive!'
Twirling leaves with tiny glee,
Cheering on the bumblebee.

Ants hold meetings, hats askew,
Debating if they'll paint it blue.
While ladybugs strike silly poses,
As flowers giggle, off it goes!

A hedgehog spills tea on the ground,
While rabbits bounce, joy unbound.
The thistles snicker with each breeze,
Making riddles with such ease.

In this underbrush of sound,
Nature's punchlines all around.
With every leaf and every stir,
Life's a joke; let laughter blur!

The Music of Lost Footfalls

Footsteps shuffle on the leaf,
Squirrels hide, oh what a thief!
The wind hums songs of the past,
As giggling toads jump fast.

A fox tiptoes with a grin,
With funny hats upon his chin.
Bunnies dance in a line,
Playing tag while feeling fine.

Sticks snap louder than a drum,
Pine cones tumble, what a thrum!
Trees sway to the beat they make,
Time for laughing after breaks.

When nature plays its merry tune,
Laughter twirls beneath the moon.
So join the waltz of bushes, trees,
For here unfolds the sweetest breeze.

The Inward Song of the Glade

In the midst of trees so tall,
A squirrel slipped, gave a squall.
Bouncing off a branch so spry,
Landed straight in a pie!

Laughter rings between the barks,
As frogs perform their tiny larks.
A raccoon winks with glee,
Stealing snacks from the big oak tree.

The breeze whispers secrets to the leaves,
While a porcupine cleverly weaves.
Dancing chipmunks steal the show,
As grass bugs also join the flow.

Nature's quirks become the stage,
Where every critter knows its page.
In the glade, the laughter flows,
Even when the clumsy crow toes!

Nature's Gentle Cadence

The robin sings a silly tune,
While bees buzz 'round in a ball like a swoon.
A bear attempts to do a jig,
And stumbles upon a giant twig.

A rabbit hops with style and flair,
But trips over its magic hare.
What a sight, the glade ignites,
With nature's dance under the lights.

A ladybug wears a tiny crown,
Taking turns to spin and frown.
The deer giggle in the night,
As fireflies twinkle with delight.

In this forest, joy takes flight,
Every creature, just feels right.
Moments shared, a laughter grand,
In this whimsical, leafy land.

The Heartbeat of the Forest

A turtle tried to race a hare,
But lost his shoes somewhere in there.
Instead of running, he just sat,
And made a friend of an old fat cat.

The winds play songs on high,
As owls hoot by with a winked eye.
But watch out, here comes the snail,
Singing off-tune with a colorful tale.

The sunbeams laugh, the shadows tease,
While branches sway in the evening breeze.
A woodpecker taps in a funny beat,
Joining in with the squirrel's feat.

In every thump, in every cheer,
Nature's laughter draws us near.
With antics pure, fun's never ceased,
In this wild, joyful feast!

Veils of Mist and Memory

In the mist, a ghostly sheep,
Wanders 'round—it cannot leap!
It trips on dew with a little bleat,
And laughs aloud at its own feet.

The wind with whispers plays a game,
Hinting secrets that are quite lame.
While foxes plot their next big joke,
Fooling all with a puffed up smoke.

A wise old owl shares a silly riddle,
Trying to jest, while hooting a little.
The trees all snicker, the leaves do sway,
As nature laughs at the bright day.

Veils of fun float soft and light,
Dancing around until the night.
In this glade, the humor's rife,
A playful dance, the heart of life!

Tales from the Verdant Heart

In the woods where squirrels chatter,
A dancing frog slips on a platter.
He lands with grace, all soaked in dew,
The trees all laugh, what's he to do?

A wise old owl hoots out a tune,
As raccoons dance under the moon.
A turtle spins, he's feeling spry,
"Hey, that's my shell!" the snail slips by!

The bushes rustle with jest and play,
As chipmunks plot their grand buffet.
With cakes of acorns piled up high,
They'll feast and laugh till morning nigh.

In this place where weird tales twine,
The weasel wears a fancy line.
"Next time I'm picking berries red,
I'll stack them high upon my head!"

Resonance of Nature's Breath

Out in the glen where moss does sway,
A mischievous breeze leads critters astray.
A deer on skates slips and glides,
While notebook frogs write joyful guides.

The blossoms giggle, tickling the bees,
"Why do you buzz? Just chill, if you please!"
A hedgehog strums a guitar so fine,
As crickets join in, and all feels divine.

A badger dons a tutu bright,
Swaying and twirling with sheer delight.
"Tonight, we celebrate!" he boldly declared,
But tripped on his tail—now that's what he shared!

In this realm where laughs entwine,
Each creature adds a twist, a sign.
"Next year," said the mouse, with a chuckle so clear,
"Let's throw a dance and invite a deer!"

The Enchanted Sylva

Beneath the boughs all thick and green,
A bear in shades pulls off a scene.
He slaps his paws, shakes a leg,
And dances circles 'round a keg!

The rabbits join with thumps and hops,
While grasshoppers do flip-flop stops.
A wise old fox with a hat so tall,
Reads out loud to the merry thrall.

"Have you heard the joke of the pine?
It says he's just too straight to dine!"
The laughter rings through every claire,
As all the fauna gather and share.

And when the sun creeps in to play,
They toast to friendship at the close of day.
A magical place where good vibes reign,
In the enchanted sylva, joy won't wane!

Threads of Light in the Green

In fields clad bright with sunlit sheen,
A chicken danced—oh, what a scene!
With clucks so loud and feathers bright,
It's the wildest party on a summer night.

A hedgehog spins, he's really slick,
Wearing a hat—what a cheeky trick!
While all the leaves join in the fun,
Throwing shades of laughter 'til day is done.

A lizard struts in flamboyant style,
"Let's do the worm!" he shouts with a smile.
The frogs croak back, "We'll join in too!"
As laughter bounces under skies so blue.

When twilight settles, colors blend,
As night descends on every friend.
They promise this laughter will remain,
Threads of joy, just like the rain!

The Forest's Timeless Lullaby

In a grove where squirrels play,
A raccoon sings the day away.
His notes are sharp, a comical spree,
With branches swaying like a glee.

The owls hoot with eyes so wide,
While turtles stop to take a ride.
They waddle slow, a dance so crude,
In nature's game, they're seldom rude.

A chipmunk juggles acorns near,
While rabbits join to wave and cheer.
A laughter spills where shadows fall,
In woodsy antics, there's fun for all.

A breeze tosses leaves in a whirl,
As deer and foxes spin and twirl.
In this haven of quirky delight,
The forest holds laughter in flight.

Reflections in the Leafy Embrace

Beneath the canopy so bright,
A raccoon's hat brings pure delight.
He prances round in silly style,
As bushes jiggle, laugh, and smile.

The bees hum tunes of sweet dessert,
While frogs in ponds wear little shirts.
They croak along in a crazy beat,
Spilling froggy rhymes at their feet.

Mice host parties up in the trees,
Swinging on branches with the breeze.
They tell tall tales of cheese galore,
And whiskers twitch at the folklore.

In a patch of grass, the ants all squinch,
Throwing a bash with a little pinch.
With tiny hats and crumbs to spare,
A woodland fête, full of flair!

The Spirit of the Woodland Realm

A fox in shades does strut and prance,
With squirrels joining in the dance.
Twigs snap under their happy feet,
As laughter rings through groovy beat.

The bunnies hop in synchronized glee,
With floppy ears, they chart the spree.
A turtle's shell becomes a stage,
For songs that calm the wildest rage.

Legends tell of mischief's trait,
When every toad sings "What's your fate?"
With every leap, they wink and smile,
In this green glen, stay for a while.

So here in woods, with trees so tall,
The woodland spirit beckons all.
Join in the fun, heed nature's call,
Where laughter echoes, big and small.

Voices Beneath the Boughs

Under leaves where shadows mingle,
A choir of crickets starts to jingle.
With fireflies wearing tiny hats,
They sing of nuts and playful spats.

A lizard slips with flair and charm,
While hedgehogs prickle, not alarm.
They share the stage, all bright and bold,
And make up tales that must be told.

With every rustle, giggles burst,
As mushrooms sprout in playful thirst.
The forest floor, a comedy show,
Where every creature steals the flow.

So if you wander through these woods,
Join in the fun, as laughter should.
For in this realm of leafy glee,
The spirit of charm will run free.

Sylvan Reverberations

In the woods, a squirrel leaps high,
Chasing shadows, oh my, oh my.
A rabbit, smug, steals a glance,
Saying, "Catch me if you dare to dance!"

The owls hoot in hilarious tunes,
While dancing bees wear tiny loons.
A deer slips on leaves, oh what a sight,
Rolling down, a furry delight!

The foxes laugh, they start to tease,
With acorns flying like silly whiz.
They claim that trees have gossip to share,
With every rustle, there's laughter in air!

A tortoise sighs, "Why run at all?
I'll outsmart you, just wait for the fall!"
The woods chuckle, in leafy delight,
In this fun-filled glade, all's just right!

Songs of the Ancient Trees

The trees hum tunes of yesteryear,
With roots that wiggle, they sway and cheer.
A woodpecker's drum joins the beat,
As branches dance, a rhythmic treat!

Beneath a bough, a badger sings,
With notes that flop, like broken wings.
Says the crow, with a caw so clear,
"Join the party, don't be a deer!"

The sunbeams giggle through shimmering leaves,
Tickling ferns like playful thieves.
All join in, in a harmonious fit,
Oh what a place, where laughter won't quit!

A raccoon twirls in sparkly shoes,
While pine cones roll with a silly snooze.
In this ancient realm of comedic cheer,
The tall trees laugh, the coast is clear!

Murmurs Beneath the Canopy

Beneath the leaves, whispers abound,
A frog's croak sends ripples around.
"Did you hear what the winds just said?
It's quite a tale, feels like I'm misled!"

The crickets chirp in a joking tone,
While a sleepy snail claims the throne.
"Race me, race me!" a chipmunk shouts,
Though everyone knows he's full of doubts!

The shadows play tag, dart here and there,
A dance of delight in the sun's warm glare.
"Who left that snack by the old oak tree?"
A squirrel exclaims, "Not me, not me!"

All frolic together, with flair and glee,
Crafting memories beneath each tree.
In this forest of mirth, they find their bliss,
Every rustle a giggle, and no moment missed!

Hushed Secrets Among the Foliage

Among the leaves, secrets abound,
A butterfly grins, then spins around.
"Did you hear the tale of the tripping hare?
He fell in a pond, oh what a scare!"

A wise old tortoise guffaws on a log,
While nearby, a frantic jumping frog.
"I'm late, I'm late!" he yells with fright,
"Must hop faster through this leafy night!"

With whispers of whimsy, the branches tease,
The mice play poker beneath the trees.
"Who's got acorns or tiny seeds?"
Laughter erupts, fulfilling their needs!

Each rustle, each giggle, in leafy delight,
As nature conspires to keep spirits bright.
Hushed secrets shared in the soft, cool air,
In this playful grove, none have a care!

Timeless Songs of the Sylvan Realm

In the woods where the squirrels dance,
A rabbit sings a silly prance.
The owls hoot a quirky tune,
As the sun rises, bright as June.

Frogs croak in a raucous choir,
Their voices rising ever higher.
A deer joins in with a jig,
While raccoons spin like a big rig.

The breeze giggles through the trees,
As whispered secrets tease the leaves.
Beneath the pines, laughter swells,
With tales that every critter tells.

And when the night begins to creep,
The fireflies wake from their sleep.
They twinkle like stars on the ground,
In this funny glade, joy abounds.

Reflections in the Verdant Boughs

A chipmunk wears a tiny hat,
He struts before a sleeping cat.
With each step, he trips and falls,
Yet laughs it off, and proudly calls.

The trees are swaying, feeling bold,
They gossip tales of days of old.
A jester's cap upon a pine,
Whispers jokes that age can't define.

In the shade, rabbits play charades,
While foxes plot their grand escapades.
A mirror pond reflects their glee,
As they splash water, wild and free.

When moonlight casts its silver glow,
From the bushes, a wise owl will show.
He hoots a riddle meant for laughs,
As merry woodland drafts its drafts.

Lullabies of the Lush Thicket

A sloth sings soft, but out of tune,
His voice would make a garden swoon.
Yet every note brings joy anew,
As butterflies twirl in the dew.

Foxes find a cozy bed,
With pillows stacked beneath their head.
They dream of cheese and dancing cheese,
In a slumber filled with giggles and wheezes.

The owls decide to throw a bash,
Inviting all with a mighty splash.
They dance around till the break of light,
In the thicket where the fun is right.

A final bash, at dawn they sing,
Of all the joy that woodland brings.
And just as day begins to rise,
They toast and laugh beneath the skies.

Traces of Twilight's Embrace

The twilight hums a fickle song,
As crickets chirp their night so strong.
A badger dons a fancy coat,
And leads the crowd with a little boat.

Bats practice flips in the cool air,
While beetles hold a grand affair.
With tiny hats and tiny tails,
They march as if on tiny trails.

The moonlight plays with shadows deep,
Where frogs swim fast in their leap.
A turtle spins in merry glee,
While laughter rolls from tree to tree.

As stars begin their twinkling dance,
The night wraps all in a joyful trance.
For in this glade of friendship and fun,
The stories linger, never done.

The Tranquil Essence of the Woods

In the woods where trees like gossip sway,
Squirrels skitter by with nuts on display.
A deer trips over roots, oh what a sight!
The forest giggles, it's a slapstick night.

Mushrooms dance in circles, twirling with glee,
While a turtle races, 'Come catch up with me!'
The raccoons are plotting a midnight feast,
Where all are invited, even the least.

Beneath the branches, wise owls take bets,
On who will trip next, or win little debts.
A fox wears a cape, thinks he's a big shot,
But who wears it best is the one that they've caught.

As sunlight drips down like honey from trees,
The squirrels discuss their new strategies.
With laughter and games, they share their delight,
For in silly woods, joy fills every night.

Woven Echoes of Forest Life

In the thicket where shadows play peek-a-boo,
Bunnies giggle softly in their fluffy crew.
A chatty crow squawks, 'Hey, watch your toes!'
As the brambles weave tales of secrets and woes.

The porcupine dreams of a prickly romance,
While bears try their luck at a waltzing dance.
With each awkward twirl, a cloud of snickers,
The dance floor shakes with their fuzzy flickers.

Old trees lean close, sharing stories of yore,
Of hares who once dared to outsmart the lore.
A wise turtle grins, slow and quite sly,
He knows that their plans often just flop and die.

When nightfall descends, the stars come to play,
Mice set up a stage for their grand cabaret.
With cheese for their scripts and acorns as light,
The laughter resounds till the dawn's early sight.

Secrets of the Canopied Path

In the woods where the squirrels play,
They hide my lunch, oh what a day!
A raccoon laughs with a cheeky grin,
As I chase my sandwich, where to begin?

Frogs conspiring in a little band,
Croaking jokes that no one planned.
A turtle slowly joins the fun,
Saying, "I'm fast? Well, not quite, hon!"

Mice are plotting, oh what a fright,
Flipping pancakes just for spite.
The trees are giggling, branches sway,
As if they know it's a silly day!

So in this glade, where laughter grows,
Under the shade, anything goes!
With every rustle, a joke unfolds,
In secret pathways, laughter molds.

Soft Echoing Steps Through Underbrush

A rabbit hops, with shoes too tight,
Complaining, "This just isn't right!"
The leaves respond with a chuckling sound,
As he trips over a mound!

Foxes gossip in the green-lit glade,
"Did you hear what the owl has made?"
Tree trunks shake, while I can't see,
The punchline waits, just behind a bee!

A deer, a dancer, moves with grace,
Only to stumble and fall on her face.
"Don't get clumsy in nature's dance!"
The mushrooms giggle as they take a stance.

Each footfall is a comical sound,
A symphony where joy is found.
With every misstep, a tale to tell,
In this underbrush, all is well!

Lattice of Life in the Understory

Beneath the leaves, a party brews,
The ants in line wear tiny shoes.
Throwing confetti made from bread,
While a snail grumbles, "I won't be wed!"

Mushrooms hosting a wacky show,
A dance-off brewed from down below.
The shadows watch, they sway and clap,
"Is he dancing? Or taking a nap?"

Snakes tell tales, they can't be true,
Of a majestic fish, dressed in blue.
Squirrels throw acorns, like they're in flight,
Their laughs echo as day turns to night.

So under the trees, secrets weave,
In this lattice, it's hard to believe.
With life's little quirks, the laughter stays,
In nature's hands, our hearts are ablaze!

Ballad of the Whispering Leaves

A leaf fell down and said, 'Oh dear!'
"I'll start a band, who wants to cheer?"
It beckoned to the crickets nearby,
Who dropped their tunes, let's give it a try!

Breezes blow and swirl around,
As the laughter of branches can be found.
One tree shimmies, giving a twist,
"Don't be shy! Join in the list!"

The wind joins in with a playful breeze,
Tickling trees, bringing hearts to ease.
Frogs croak choruses, oh what a treat,
While worms wiggle to the upbeat beat!

So listen close to the soft applause,
In this woodland, humor has no flaws.
With every rustle, a joke takes flight,
In the laughter of nature, all feels right!

The Soft Symphony of the Grove

Bubbles of laughter from trees delight,
Squirrels play tag, oh what a sight!
Sunbeams twinkle, dance like they're free,
While flowers gossip with each bumblebee.

Mushrooms wear hats, oh what a show,
Dancing to rhythms the critters know.
A snail slips by, on a quest so grand,
But moves like molasses—oh, isn't life bland?

The wind cracks jokes, rustles the leaves,
Telling tall tales that nobody believes.
A frog croaks a pun, it's truly divine,
As shadows dance joyfully, keeping time.

In this grove of giggles, where joy's on parade,
Nature's a comedian, never afraid.
So come join the fun, hear the jolly refrain,
And leave with a smile, not dropping a grain.

Whispers of the Canopied Glade

In a glade where the sun likes to play peek-a-boo,
The flowers are whispering secrets to you.
A chipmunk with style struts like a star,
While birds debate who's the best singer thus far.

The moss on the ground is a fluffy green couch,
Where rabbits hold court, making wisecracks with slouch.

A butterfly flutters, it's fashion week here,
With colors so bold, you cannot help but cheer.

Squirrels write dramas, their actors take flight,
Arguing over whose acorn is right.
And under the branches, a snail shakes with glee,
For all of their chaos makes great comedy!

Nature's a stage and the crowd is a hive,
Where every small creature feels lively and alive.
So laugh with the leaves and giggle with grace,
In this whimsical haven, find your happy place.

Nature's Ethereal Dialogue

A dance of delight in the rustling breeze,
Where trees crack up as they tickle the leaves.
The brook sings softly, its rhythm so fine,
While a porcupine updates his meme timeline.

Frogs trade their jokes by the shimmering pond,
And ducks waddle by like a well-rehearsed bond.
With each little quack, there's laughter around,
As mushrooms giggle snugly beneath the ground.

The butterflies flutter, in glittery glee,
Declaring it's party time, come join the spree!
Their wings make confetti that floats everywhere,
And ants in tuxedos are dancing in pairs.

A wise old owl hoots out riddles at night,
Telling critters to hold onto their fright.
In this light-hearted world, woes drift away,
As laughter and joy are the stars of the day.

Threads of Stories in the Leaves

The leaves are storytellers, weaving their tales,
Of beasts, and of mishaps, and whimsical trails.
The wind carries giggles through branches that sway,
As creatures share secrets in a playful display.

A raccoon dons glasses, reading with flair,
While a turtle bakes cupcakes without a care.
A rabbit in bowtie gives speeches on grass,
With the frogs as his audience, laughing en masse.

The daisies are jesters, their petals are bright,
They fool the tall trees when managing height.
And the sun peeks down, with a smirk on his face,
At the antics below, in this silly place.

In this vibrant haven, where laughter is free,
Nature's own comedy is truly the key.
So skip through the glades, hear the whimsical sounds,
And dance with the flora where funny abounds.

The Soundtrack of the Wild

A squirrel with a flair for pop,
Dances on branches, can't ever stop.
The birds join in, a feathered band,
While bunnies tap dance on the sand.

A raccoon starts beatboxing right near,
With lyrics that tickle the ear.
The breeze carries tunes, all around,
Nature's concert, oh what a sound!

Trees sway with laughter, leaves in a spin,
Each rustling whisper, a giggle within.
Even the flowers sway to the beat,
Joining this party, oh so sweet!

So come, take a seat, join this affair,
The wild has music that's beyond compare.
With every chirp and bounce in the night,
The forest is laughing, oh what a sight!

Melodic Tendrils of Verdancy

In the dewy dawn, the grass starts to hum,
With worms doing jazz, oh, so much fun!
The daisies join in, a bloom-tastic cheer,
While ants perform ballet, quite sincere.

The caterpillars strum on leafy guitars,
While ladybugs beat drums and shout, 'Hoorahs!'
A waltz of the wild, in every direction,
Nature's own dance, with perfect perfection.

Breezes shimmy, they twist and they twirl,
Tickling the branches, making them whirl.
With every rustle, a catchy new tune,
Even the moonlight joins in by noon.

So listen closely, to this tune divine,
In the tendrils of green, with rhythm entwined.
It's a symphony made of giggles and glee,
Nature's sweet melody, wild and free!

Tales from the Whispering Pines

The pines share secrets, so silly and bright,
'The rain danced with frogs, what a quirky sight!'
A woodpecker laughs at the tales being spun,
As shadows of squirrels get bathed in the sun.

When the sunbeams tickle the tree trunks so wide,
The branches shake hands as they giggle with pride.
A breeze carries stories, oh, what a delight,
Of raccoons who raid parties with snacks late at night.

Chipmunks are scheming their nut-hiding fate,
While hedgehogs spin tales about their last date.
The rabbits throw shade at the turtle's slow pace,
As the owls shake their heads, a wise look on their face.

So gather around, hear the pines spin their yarn,
For every tall story holds a sprinkle of charm.
In the heart of the wood, laughter fills every nook,
A whimsical saga, just open a book!

Vestiges of the Enchanted Glen

In the glen where the sprites used to play,
A frog croaks jokes that brighten the day.
Mushrooms giggle and sway to the sound,
In this magic corner, joy is unbound.

The fairies are sly, they prance and they sneak,
Pull pranks on the owls, oh what a peak!
With twirls and swirls, they scatter and dive,
A dance-off erupts, they feel so alive.

Foxes tell tales of adventures so grand,
Rustling through brambles, a merry band.
The leaves play along, each rustle a cheer,
In the glen, it's all laughter, nothing to fear.

So step lightly here, where the fun never ends,
With friends all around, let the silliness blend.
In the magical glen, let your spirit ascend,
A treasure of laughter, your heart will commend!

The Song of Hollowed Trunks

In the hollowed tree, a squirrel sings,
With acorns as drums, it dances and swings.
A raccoon joins in, all furry and spry,
While owls roll their eyes, as they hoot a sly.

The beetles tap dance on roots underground,
As the tree trunk grooves to the silly sound.
The fungi laugh loud, their caps all a-flop,
In the glade of the silly, the joy never stops.

A chipmunk spins tales, full of twist and shout,
Of ghosts in the branches who giggle and pout.
The breeze shakes the leaves, making all topsy-turvy,
In the dance of the woods, it's all just so swervy.

With bark outfits on, the trees sway and twirl,
In a foxtrot of fun, as their branches unfurl.
The forest erupts, a whimsical spree,
In the realm of the woods, where we laugh with glee.

Mysteries of the Swaying Boughs

The branches twist tales, in the light of the moon,
Of owls who play poker, a nightly festoon.
The wind joins the game, with a chuckle and whistle,
While shadows take bets, in the dark with a gristle.

A deer with a bowtie prances on by,
Counting the stars, as they flicker and fly.
In a contest with foxes, who wink and who prance,
The night's full of giggles, a laugh-filled dance.

The boughs wink mysteriously, swaying with grace,
As the moon's silly rays splatter light on their face.
The critters all gather, with a cheer and a clap,
To ponder what's next in their nighttime mishap.

At dawn they disperse in a jolly parade,
With twinkling-eyed wonders, their plans never fade.
In the sway of the trees, there's mischief to find,
A conclave of laughter, uniquely designed.

Reflections on the Forest Floor

On the floor of the woods where the sun's rays peek,
The mushrooms all giggle, a chaotically chic.
With fairy dust sprinkled, they sport a grand hat,
A tea party starts, with a flask and a spat.

The bugs bring their snacks, in a jolly parade,
While beetles play chess on the soft mossy shade.
Ants stomp with a tune, they start up the beat,
Drawing in leaf-frogs who dance on their feet.

With puddles like mirrors, reflecting the fun,
The shadows are laughing, when the day's almost done.
The forest floor whispers its secrets out loud,
While critters join in, saying "Look at us, proud!"

The laughter resounds as the sun takes its bow,
All critters retire, to the night they avow.
With a wink and a smile, in the glen they shall snore,
Dreaming of mischief, yes, they'll wake for more!

Twilight's Embrace in the Grove

At twilight's soft touch, the fun begins here,
With raccoons in capes, spreading gossip and cheer.
The fireflies flicker, their lanterns ablaze,
In a darting duet, they dance through the haze.

The trees tell tall tales, with their voices so low,
Of fairies who trip, and gnomes who don't know.
A babbling brook giggles, its water all churned,
With fish leaping high, laughter learned, laughter earned.

As the night sets in, with shadows a-flop,
The critters convene, for a grand story swap.
From raccoons' capers to owls' wise jokes,
In a swirl of delight, the woodland awokes.

With twirls and with whirls, the grove's filled with glee,
In the embrace of darkness, they'll dance carefree.
With a wink and a nod, as the stars gleam above,
The grove laughs together, in joy and in love.

Whispers of the Forgotten Wood

In the woods where squirrels play,
Dancing leaves seize the day.
A rabbit slips with a wiggle and hop,
But trips on twigs and goes 'thud' with a plop.

The old owl laughs from a branch up high,
While raccoons trade tales of the moonlit sky.
'Watch my tricks!' says a chipmunk with flair,
As he stumbles and tumbles, a jester laid bare.

Crickets chirp under the bushes nearby,
Turning gossip into a musical sigh.
'Who was that fool?' asks a crow in distress,
Just as the bushes take on a big mess.

In this wood where laughter does thrive,
Each little mishap comes alive.
With a twirl and a giggle, let's raise a toast,
To the witty woods where we laugh the most.

Shadows Among Ancient Pines

In the shade where shadows play,
A clumsy fox lost his way.
He struts with pride, tail held so high,
Then trips on roots, oh my, oh my!

Squirrels chuckle at his plight,
While butterflies take off in flight.
'Look at this goof!' they snicker and tease,
As he wriggles out from the tangled trees.

A wise old tortoise, slow but keen,
Sips on dew like a king, serene.
'You should slow down,' he gives a grin,
'Life's a journey, not a race to win!'

Yet the fox bounces back, full of sass,
'Look at me now, I'm nobody's ***!'
With laughter trailing in the air,
The woods come alive with joy to share.

Secrets of the Serene Grove

Beneath the boughs so thick and green,
Lies a party unseen, so keen.
A bear, a badger, enjoying their pie,
They snicker and munch as the ants march by.

A squirrel, with a hat, looks dapper yet lost,
Tries to dance, but oh, at what cost!
He twirls and spins, gets tangled in vines,
The whole grove bursts out with chuckles and pines.

The wise owl hoots, 'What's all this fuss?'
While a raccoon, with flair, claims, 'Join us, trust!'
And as laughter fills this tranquil space,
Even the trees start to reveal a face.

With giggles and snacks under the twilight,
This secret grove knows how to delight.
So come one, come all, to join in the fun,
In the midst of this grove, we're never outdone.

Murmurs Beneath the Canopy

Beneath the leaves, a whisper so sly,
A hedgehog plans his escape, oh my!
He wiggles and squirms through the tall, lush grass,
Only to stop when he spies a big lass.

A deer, with grace, gives him a stare,
'You're not very sneaky—do you want a share?'
With a rat-a-tat laugh, he pauses and ponders,
As the forest joins in with its humid wonders.

A lumberjack's hat, a squirrel's grand prize,
He wears it with flair, oh, how he tries!
But the brim's too large; it flops on his nose,
As the woodland critters erupt with their prose.

'Let's start a band!' chirps a bold little bird,
While the hedgehog rolls back, laughing unheard.
In this green dream where the silly run free,
Nature's jesters forever will be.

Nature's Forgotten Cadence

The squirrel dances, twirls around,
With acorns flying, all abound.
The owl hoots a silly tune,
While raccoons join, quite out of tune.

The trees giggle, branches sway,
As sunlight tries to join the play.
A fox trips over roots that grow,
And everyone just laughs, you know!

A rabbit wearing shades so bright,
Claims he can hop to dizzy height.
But stumbles, lands in a patch of grass,
Where daisies bloom and critters laugh!

The wind whispers jokes, so clever and spry,
As butterflies flutter, spreading good cheer high.
Nature's stage is set, the applause begins,
In this wild world, everyone wins!

Whispers in the Leafy Sanctuary

In a leafy nook where things get weird,
A turtle shouts, though he's quite feared.
His friends all giggle, as he takes a stand,
Declaring he'll wrestle a vacant land!

The birds crack jokes from high up above,
While the shy hedgehog learns to shove.
With tiny laughs and big belly rolls,
They're the party crowd with heart and souls!

A chipmunk juggles with nuts and a sprout,
But drops them all, calling out, "No doubt!"
A skunk nearby snickers, what a sight,
He tries to help but runs off in fright!

The shadows stretch, the sun dips low,
As nature's antics steal the show.
In this sanctuary, laughter rings clear,
A place where joy and fun appear!

Secrets of the Mossy Pathway

On the mossy path where secrets hide,
A snail tells tales, moving with pride.
His friends all gather, eyes open wide,
   As he spins a yarn of a daring ride!

A ladybug prances, all dressed in red,
Chasing her dreams, with a leaf for a bed.
But the wind sneezes, sends her in a twirl,
She giggles and spins, giving life a whirl!

A toad croaks riddles that cause a laugh,
While mushrooms dance in an earthy bath.
They conga along, though wobbly at best,
Creating a scene that you can't contest!

In the twilight glow, the fun never halts,
The forest is filled with nature's exalts.
From silly stories to playful themes,
This mossy pathway is bursting at the seams!

Memories in the Lush Understory

In a vibrant thicket, where shadows play,
A goat sings loudly, come join the fray!
His songs are goofy, off-key, and bold,
While bunnies hop close, enjoying the gold.

The ferns share tales of days long past,
When wild weeds danced, oh, such a blast!
They chuckle together, under sun's embrace,
In this lush haven, joy takes its place.

A lizard slides down, smooth as can be,
Telling all critters, "Just look at me!"
A tumble, a roll, he lands in a patch,
With giggles and snickers, they all catch!

The saxophone trees play a soulful tune,
As critters gather, beneath the moon.
In the understory, laughter swells high,
Creating memories that never say goodbye!

Serendipity in the Canopy's Dance

The squirrels hold a disco night,
With acorns flying left and right.
Branches sway to nature's beat,
While critters groove on tiny feet.

A fox arrives in sparkly shoes,
He twirls and spins, it's quite the cruise.
The birds chirp tunes with perfect pitch,
As bees buzz by, they form a switch.

The owls look on with judging stares,
While raccoons practice silly glares.
But laughter rings through leaves so green,
As forest friends dance in between.

All join the fun, no fuss, no frowns,
Under the shade, nobody downs.
In this great glade, all spirits lift,
Nature's dance, the funniest gift.

Dappled Light and Shadowed Truths

Sunbeams peek through leafy seams,
While fawns plot pranks and silly schemes.
The breeze carries whispers, a playful tease,
As mushrooms giggle beneath the trees.

Each shadow holds a secret grin,
The laughter echoes, let the fun begin.
A rabbit hops with flair and style,
As turtles join in with a chuckling smile.

The wise old owl finds it absurd,
To join in jokes without a word.
Yet, he chuckles, all fluff and might,
At jokes exchanged in the fading light.

The sun sets slow, the moon takes charge,
With a twinkle and glow, the night's at large.
But in this glade, the fun won't cease,
For laughter reigns, it's nature's peace.

Melodies of the Whispering Winds

A gentle breeze plays hide and seek,
With flowers dancing, unique and chic.
The wind hums tunes, a whimsical song,
As trees sway along, bouncing along.

Bunnies prance with rhythm in their hearts,
While the toads add beats with tiny farts.
The mushrooms sway, giving it a try,
As crickets chirp, you can't deny.

The forest sings in harmony,
A hilarious symphony, wild and free.
Though nature plays, no one's too shy,
To share a laugh as the moments fly.

Together they sway, in rhythmic delight,
Under the stars shining so bright.
In this woodland band, life's the best spin,
With every note, they all break in.

The Forest's Hidden Memories

In the woods where secrets dwell,
Old trees whisper tales to tell.
A squirrel claims to be a king,
While rabbits laugh, adding zing.

The raccoons hold a meeting grand,
With plans to swipe the picnic band.
The trees nod wise, they've seen it all,
From silly dances to the fall.

A past of hijinks, an autumn feast,
With every critter, to say the least.
The wise old owl, in twilight's glow,
Shares stories of friends long ago.

Nostalgia wraps like morning mist,
As laughter echoes, they can't resist.
These memories bloom like wildflowers,
In the glade, it's fun for hours.

www.ingramcontent.com/pod-product-compliance
Lightning Source LLC
Chambersburg PA
CBHW072145200426
43209CB00051B/666